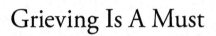
Grieving Is A Must

Grieving Is A Must

A Christian Approach to Coping
with the Loss of a Loved One

Rose Flemming-Nyako, Ph.D.

GRIEVING IS A MUST
A CHRISTIAN APPROACH TO COPING WITH THE LOSS OF A LOVED ONE

iUniverse books may be ordered through booksellers or by contacting:

iUniverse
1663 Liberty Drive
Bloomington, IN 47403
www.iuniverse.com
1-800-Authors (1-800-288-4677)

ISBN: 978-1-5320-0434-6 (sc)
ISBN: 978-1-5320-0435-3 (e)

Library of Congress Control Number: 2016912708

Print information available on the last page.

iUniverse rev. date: 09/22/2016

A Special Dedication to a Special Person,

In Loving Memory of My Friend.

Fannette Roberta Fisher

Thank You for leaving me the fingerprints of grace on my life. For your kindness and devotion and for your endless support when I needed a safe haven for my son Kofi. You opened your doors and cared for him. Your selflessness will always be remembered.

Dedication

To my mother, Sarah Louise Flemming, who provided me with so much love. My Mommy was my rock, my pillar of strength, my nurturer, my rescuer, and my protector.

Her strength and courage in the fight against cancer (Leukemia) inspired me to pursue my education and follow my dreams to keep writing so that I could give her this book as my gift of our eternal love.

When we all get to heaven where you are, what a day of rejoicing that will be.

IN LOVING MEMORY

George Flemming (Daddy)

Evangelist Esther Richardson (Grandmother)

Robert Donaldson (Uncle)

George Flemming, Jr. (Brother)

Mark Flemming (Brother)

Michael Flemming (Brother)

Andrew and Mary Smith (Children's Godparents)

Dr. Richard Appia Nyako, M.D.

CONTENTS

ACKNOWLEDGEMENTS

A book may have a single author or several authors, but many valued people make its foundation possible. I have been blessed with countless glorious friends, family members, colleagues, and spiritual advisors. I would like to express my very great appreciation. First, I would like to thank my family —my sons: Dwayne Flemming and Twumasi Kofi Appia Nyako, for their encouragement and support in this long process of writing this book. My brother, Gregory Flemming, for his special help, and my sisters, Cheryl Flemming-Jackson-Wilson and Deidra Flemming-McGill, for their inspiration and perseverance with me. Dr. Richard Appia Nyako, ex-husband (deceased), who purchased the computer, which enabled me to write this book. Second, Newburgh Theological Seminary Academic and Supportive staff for their on-going prayers, and guidance of my pursuit of my Doctoral Degree in Christian Counseling. Dr. Les Liebengood for taking on the task of being my Mentor/Advisor during this writing project and clarifying conceptual issues. Dr. Barbara Norman for her guidance with finding important references and research.

I am particularly grateful to Sister Linda Ross, for her proofreading and countless ways in the book production. April Payne, a friend. Elder Charity McCottrell, Henley, and Tilleth Walters who provided spiritual nurturing. Foluke Joyce Omosule, a colleague, for her useful and constructive recommendations on this project. Evangelist Ruby Johnson, a childhood friend and spiritual advisor, she answered my calls in the middle of the night when I had an idea or a thought for this project. Her continuous prayers were much welcomed.

Finally, I thank the Grace and Mercy of my Lord and Savior, Jesus who walks with me every day of my life.

INTRODUCTION

The idea of this book came about as a newly graduated Ph.D. I was, like many other graduates, concerned about creating a book and publishing one of the most hard-working task in my life, my dissertation.

Over thirty –five years of my career in Nursing and Counseling, I worked with individuals and families who were grieving due to the loss of their loved ones. As a nurse, often I was responsible for medicating people who was dying and in pain, to alleviate their pain. I was also involved with the responsibility for breaking the news to family members of the passing of their loved one, and gathering available appropriate resources for families. As a counselor, I worked with individuals and their families with coping skills of the death of their loved ones. My counseling skills include, anticipatory grief, practicing the use of the stages of death and dying by Kubler Ross as referenced in this book, as well as dealing with complicated grief issues.

GRIEVING IS A MUST addresses loss as a universal experience. Losing the loss of a loved one involves fundamental elements of living, which is shared by all people regardless of social and cultural differences amongst them.

All humans are born, all humans grow, all humans experience various different emotions throughout their lives, and all humans die; it is indisputable that we all will go through these fundamental biological processes as human beings. That is what I would describe as the "Universal Human Experience." This book contains help on how to cope with the loss of a loved one in a Christian and wholesome way.

Some people are good at hiding their emotions and when grief comes along, it is just another emotion to bury. Wearing your feelings on your sleeve or asking for help, showing weakness, letting someone else see the most covered part of you is not an easy task.

For the most part of my young adult life, it hasn't been easy for me to open up myself to others. I am the fifth child of seven, yet somehow I became somewhat of a loner. Not one to readily share my feelings and experiences with others. At the age of twenty-seven, when my "mommy" died, I became even more withdrawn. I was afraid to turn to people for comfort. I was unsure of what I really wanted from them. Couldn't they see I was saturated in pain? Couldn't they see I wasn't asking for help? How do you let them in your world, the secret part of your life? If I don't let them in, will I be able to handle this pain alone? The fear of falling apart can be consuming.

As time passed by I was eventually able to open up to a Christian elderly woman who had no academic training but she had a sound relationship with God and she readily shared her spiritual experiences with her higher power. This was my first introduction to Christian Counseling.

I learned that no matter how unexpected or predictable, death flusters us to the core. The pain is unpreventable. There can be joy, peace, and comfort through your grieving journey. Time does not heal all by itself, but the way we use the time that is available to us can help us to heal and grow. I spent time every day learning more and more about how to lean and depend on a power far above man or woman. The power of God began to consume me as my relationship with Him developed. I began to understand that I could do nothing on my own without the help of God. With much prayer, meditation, and reading comforting words from God, I began to feel more secure about this thing called grief. I was learning, it's ok to grieve and in time, healing will refresh your spirit.

As I sought God more for guidance, grief recovery became real to me, I flourished into a person who can open up to others and share the intimate side of me and listen to others.

CHAPTER 1

The Experience of
Separation by Death

Developing a relationship with loved ones involves a process of growth and development with that person. Often people commit themselves to one another- they share time with the other, they keep appointments, they talk up the partner in conversations with other people, they provide emotional support in time of distress, and they give gifts and transfer resources to each other. They share meaningful events that take place in each other's lives. The time we share with our loved ones may be brief or long-term; however, some bonding develops:

> Human bonding is the process of development of a close, interpersonal relationship. Bonding is a mutual, interactive process, and is different liking. Bonding typically refers to the process of attachment that develops between romantic partners, close friends, or parents and children. This bond is characterized by emotions such as affection and trust. Any two people who spend time together may form a bond. Male bonding refers to the establishment of relationships between men through shared activities that often exclude females. The term

female bonding refers to the formation of close personal relationships between women.[1]

Christians develop relationships based on their beliefs, which are bible based. The bible teaches Christians how to form a deep relationship with God and foster the knowledge of His Word in developing a bond with others.

When we separate from the physical presence of a loved one through death, the process of grieving occurs. Most of us are not prepared for it and have not been taught in a positive way what to do with this event. Based on our belief system, some believe there is nothing after death and this may be quite frightening. Others believe in heaven of some kind and maybe a hell, and may be quite fearful of how they may be judged to be worthy of one or the other. Separation from all you know, from your family and friends, and leaving behind all that you hold dear to your heart can cause fear.

Although the grieving process is personal and some aspects are different for each individual, there are certain experiences and feelings that are common to mourners in general, regardless of race, ethnicity, culture, or religion. Many factors affect how someone grieves.

The Process of Grieving

Since there are many factors that influence the grieving process, it is essential to view some of these factors. They include, but are not limited to suddenness of death, family relationships, and the number of children in the bereaved family, the relationship between the person who died and the mourner and the support systems of the bereaved.

How we handle the loss of a parent, sibling, child, family members, and friends can be one of the most difficult challenges to face. Even though death is a natural part of life, we still can be overcome by shock and bewilderment, leading to extended periods of uncertainty, sorrow, or depression. The sorrow usually diminishes in intensity as time passes, but grieving is a necessary process in order to overcome these feelings and continue to reflect on the time you shared with your loved one.

Grief takes many forms for all of us depending on a number of factors- our relationship to the person who has died, our age, our personalities, whether or not we have experienced any losses before and the number of losses in our lives. Everyone reacts differently to death and coping with grief will manifest itself in different ways:

> Your grief is a symbol of the quality of relationship you had with one who has died. Rather than trying to hide your grief, I encourage you to wear signs of it as a badge of honor. Your tears, the heaviness in your heart, and overwhelming sense of loneliness all say, This person, this marriage, this part of my life has been so important to me that nothing will ever be the same again. My grief is the last act of love I have to give, and will wear it with pride.[2]

Many people believe, "If only I were stronger, I wouldn't feel this way." However, the reality is that grieving due to a permanent separation of a loved one because of death is an expected "normal" process. There is no "normal" time for someone to grieve. No matter how old you are, where you live, or what you do for a living, it is a safe bet that you can identify with the sadness that comes along with death. However, with passage of time, good family, social support and healthy habits, most people can lessen the intensity from their loss.

The grieving process can be especially difficult as individuals attempt to explore answers to 'why', while they are also faced with the steps of healing. Understanding the emotions that accompany grief can be helpful with the healing process. However, suppressing your grief may have an untoward effect on your ability to move forward. Individuals need to understand it is imperative that they address the issue of grief. They also need to make a conscious effort to manage their actions, as the alternative can be even harder to deal with. There are many reasons individuals do not grieve after death of a loved one.

Maybe they are plagued with misconceptions about grief. Perhaps they feel like they have to be strong for others. Whatever the reasons are when people fail to grieve, the side effects of this suppressed emotion can take control of our lives, hindering us from taking control of this natural, healthy response to death.

My Personal Experience of Grieving

My personal experience of permanent separation of loved ones by death, including my grieving experience and how I coped with my loss, are the basis for me writing about this topic. I have suffered many losses in my life. Permanent separation in relationships, jobs, homes and a pet dog were part of my losses. Not to minimize those losses, but when my two brothers, my mother and father, and my grandmother of whom I had a close relationship with died within a ten year time span of one another, I felt isolated and all alone, though I had support from my children, siblings, family and friends. I grieved somewhat differently for each of these deaths.

Mostly, I felt like a piece of my tissue in my body was torn, or there was a hole in my heart. The losses left me feeling like a piece of me has been ripped from my soul and a part of me was missing. These losses triggered a grieving process that affected the way I felt about myself, my outlook on life, and how I interacted with others in my daily living, at home, work, church, and community.

I am now experiencing the anticipation of the loss of my ex-husband who is terminally ill. We too have a bond- an adult son who is developmentally challenged. Since he has been sick for a while, we are experiencing grieving while he is alive. I can only imagine that my grieving process will include how our son will respond to his loss, and implementing coping mechanisms to help him adjust to his lifestyle changes.

I especially recall when my dear mother died; she was the first of my close knitted family to have passed away. I was twenty-nine years old and though I was married with two children, my mother was still

4

my rock and my confidante. Not a day went by without us talking to one another. I relied on her unbiased support, wisdom, guidance, and love. A part of my identity was built upon her. I would repeatedly ask myself how I could go on without her.

I have always had a strong Christian foundation and faith. As a graduate student in counseling, I learned how to apply my faith to my practice of helping others. Now the true test would be how to apply my faith to this devastating reality in my life. I had learned about Elizabeth Kubler-Ross while in nursing undergraduate school. As a follower of the Kubler-Ross Model, I knew that not only could I not escape my grief, but also that grieving is a natural healthy process.

In addition to understanding, listening to others talk about their grief experience, reading about it and experiencing the physical, emotional, and spiritual symptoms, one must understand it takes time to heal. In fact, I discovered there was little preparation for grief that accompanied death. The sharing of hugs and kisses, laughter, crying, phone calls, outings, and family gatherings with your loved one suddenly comes to a halt. We go through life with evolving changes and adaptation to our circumstances. We learn to readjust to our surroundings, our roles and to each other. We have a sense of control and purpose as we constantly redefine ourselves.

When our relationships come to a halt because of separation by death, it creates another personal redefining of ourselves. We all may shed a different light on our experiences with our grieving process, but we all share a common goal of struggling with how to move forward rather than become trapped with the inability to control our mental health. I always thought I was in control of my emotions and I could readily identify unhealthy behavior changes- I was not. With the loss of my mother, I found myself longing to have my 'mommy' back in my life. I felt that way for a long time. I stayed in the denial stage for a long time. I did not cope well with confusion either. For a while, the disbelief of my mother's death went through my mind long after she had died. My thinking was muddled, I was irritable, and it was difficult to concentrate on some things. I could only focus on our life together before she died. I suffered physical symptoms as well. I had headaches, cold chills, stomach - aches and sleepless nights.

We need to be aware that losses rarely come alone. A single death can bring many losses, some of which may not become apparent for a while. Typical losses include the presence and companionship of the person you love, some aspects of your own identity, physical and financial security, and perhaps even problems with your own health.

H. Norman Wright offers insight about the struggles of grief. "When you enter into grief, you enter the valley of shadows. There is nothing heroic or noble about grief. It is painful. It is work. It is a lingering process. But it is necessary for all kinds of losses."[3]

CHAPTER 2

When is the Right Time to Grieve?

Solomon, also known as, 'The Preacher' deals with the subject of all things happening in their own time and season, (Ecclesiastes 3:1-8, NIV):

Time for Everything

There is a time for everything, and a season for every activity under heaven:

2. a time to be born and a time to die,
   a time to plant and a time to uproot,
2. a time to kill and a time to heal,
   a time to tear down and a time to build,
4. a time to weep and a time to laugh,
   a time to mourn and a time to dance,
5. a time to scatter stones and a time to gather them,
   a time to embrace and a time to refrain,
6. a time to search and a time to give up,
   a time to keep and a time to throw away,
7. a time to tear and a time to mend,
   a time to be silent and a time to speak,

8. a time to love and a time to hate,
    a time for war and a time for peace.

Solomon clearly validates that all things, including dying and grieving, come in their own time. If it is not time, there is nothing you can do to change it. He is saying that we cannot force anything because a greater power than ourselves has control over our situations, including our mind, body, and soul.

There is no normal time for grieving. Some people start to adjust to their loss in weeks or months. For others, the grieving process is measured in years. Healing cannot be rushed or forced. Being patient with yourself and allowing the process to naturally unfold is an important step to take with healing. Grief affects each individual differently:

> Recent research has shown that intense grieving lasts from three months to a year and many people continue experiencing profound grief for two years or more. Others' response to this extended grieving process may sometimes cause people to feel there is something wrong with them or they are behaving abnormally. This is not the case. The grieving process depends on the individual's belief system, religion, life experiences and the type of loss suffered.[4]

We live in a society where we have come to believe there is a quick fix for our inconveniences or problems. For example, we cut our finger and bleed; we apply pressure and cover the wound with a tight bandage. That is the quick fix to treating a cut finger. Should the wound be deeper than we thought, and it continues to bleed, the quick fix will not heal the wound.

Grief takes as long as it takes. Some of us are faced with sudden death of a loved one. A car accident, a sudden unexpected illness or even chronic illnesses of family and friends leaves us asking the question, "How can I find relief?" Embracing the death of a loved one is not an easy task. "No living thing, in its normal state, will embrace death.

Such an embrace is viewed as aberrant, abnormal, and unnatural. Jesus proclaimed the universal norm for all living things:" I have come that you may have life, and have it more abundantly. [John 10:10]"[5]

We can begin the process of embracing the loss of a loved one by:

1. Actually experiencing the death of a loved one.
2. Understanding the basic concept and reality of physical death: we are conceived, born, live, and die.
3. We grieve and mourn death with our loved ones.
4. Examine our belief system about death and dying. Our spirituality at a time of loss can be the source of comfort. God and our faith can be our source of strength to turn to through our loss.
5. Familiarize ourselves with how other cultures cope with grieving.
6. Be open to healing.
7. Be assessing and re-evaluating our experiences and transformations through the situation.
8. Working through the stages of grief.

Frank A. Jones expounds on this type of fear:

> There is a fear of death by all human beings, yet the Bible gives us the most sure indication of what will transpire after life and also the nature of death. Human beings, however, have wondered beyond the Bible and written about death throughout all ages of man. In many Eastern cultures, there is the belief that death is not a polite subject for discussion. For many, to talk about death is to bring it on. That is their custom and belief, and they shy away from mentioning it.[6]

Unbelievers have their own faith belief system. However, they too experience the reality of death as it occurs in their lives, and they grieve.

Different Responses Different Times

Because people cope with loss in different ways, we should try to avoid judging their reactions to their loss. Some people ask the question, "Should I cry?"

There is no right or wrong way to express the pain, sorrow, and emotions of coping with the loss of a loved one. The lack of tears does not denote that one is grieving any less or that you loved the loved ones any less, nor does it mean that this lack of emotion means that the griever is having difficulty adjusting to the loss. Their body will cope in the way that is best for them. The time of grief will come and it is important to allow yourself to feel the pain.

Expressions of grief depends on a number of factors that may range from the emotional closeness of the family, how the family defines grief, the role and relationship to the deceased, and one's spiritual and psychosocial strength. Individual, family, community, and professional support may also be contributing factors to the expression of grief.

Experiencing the loss of a loved one can bring stress to our lives. We don't recognize that changes can affect our well-being. Our minds and our bodies react to these stressors. Our bodies have a way of protecting us when it is alarmed:

> Whenever we are threatened physically or psychologically, a chain of responses is set in motion to prepare us for what has been described as the "fight or flight" response. More accurately, it should be called the "fight, fright", or flight response." It's as simple as that. When we are under stress, any stress, we are prepared to attack what is threatening us, run away from it, or just go into an extreme state of fear or panic. Behind it all it is our wonderful adrenal system with its complex assortment hormones, all designed to do something or the other.[7]

Sympathetic nerves prepare the body for emergencies and stress by increasing the blood flow. These nerves become aroused as part of the fight-or-flight response, which is the body's natural reaction to real or imaginary danger.

We must be careful about the "should" and the "should not's" of grief and our reaction to our stress related grieving. This experience called "grief" is an individual journey that we all must bear eventually. What we do have in common is that our body's fight-flight response provides us with the energy reflexes and strength we may need to respond to the stressor.

Some Physical Changes That Affect Us:

- Rapid breathing, which helps get more oxygen thru-ought your body.
- Our pupils dilate so our sight is sharpened.
- Increase in heart rate to get blood and energy to the body.
- Blood pressure increases to get blood flowing faster.
- Metabolism increases to provide more energy to take on danger.
- Your muscles tense up, which prepares you to move more quickly.
- Blood sugar increases to provide more fuel for fighting or running.
- You feel exhausted, prolonged exposure to cortisol depletes your body's energy and worsen mood.

Some Emotional Changes That Affect Us:

- shock
- numbness
- disbelief
- fear
- confusion
- sadness
- crying
- irritability
- helplessness

The Relaxation Response is a state of deep rest that changes the physical and emotional responses to stress and decreases the heart rate, blood pressure, rate of breathing and muscle tension. The physical and emotional changes listed decrease.

These physical and emotional changes that may affect us during our stressful time of grieving for our loss, may also affect our behavior. There may be a change in our socialization pattern. At times, we might need our space with social contacts. Family and friends may experience a feeling of helplessness, not knowing what to do or say to the bereaved.

Our spirituality may be affected while experiencing loss. For some individuals spirituality can be a foundation of strength. Some find God through their loss. However, for others, their relationship with God may be affected. Their anger might be toward God, blaming God for their loss, pain and suffering, along with other stressors associated with their loss. Death is an event that is stress producing since we have no control over its timing, nor over the timing of our reaction and responses to our grieving. "Things that worry, scare, or frighten us, even though they only exist in our thoughts, are stress-producing because there is little we can do to fight vague, imagined threats."[8]

Western cultures are comprised of people from different cultural and religious backgrounds who react to death and experience bereavement in different ways. Their reactions to death influence length of time of grieving as does in other parts of the world, although in other parts of the world open expression of grief is not only accepted but also is to be expected. In West Africa, for example, funerals are often are delayed for a period after the death. This is often due to the status of the deceased, rituals, the financial burden of the funeral expense, and to allow family members abroad, travel time to attend funeral services. Other funerals on the same day in the same village, may also affect the grieving process.

CHAPTER 3

The Stages of Grief

When individuals suffer a major loss, they at times experience some form of grief, defined by Kubler-Ross and Kessler as "the healing process that ultimately brings us comfort in our pain."[9] Various writers, psychologist, and researchers have written about the stages of the grieving process. Although there are some discrepancies about the actual stages of grief, it is commonly known that grieving people do experience some sort of "process." Some have developed models as a tool to apply to the process of death and dying and the grief experience. The "Five stages of Grief" introduced by Dr. Elisabeth Kubler-Ross are now almost universally applied to the emotional reactions that follow our losses.

In Kubler-Ross's 1969 book on "Death and Dying", she introduced the "Five stages of Grief" which represented what a dying person might experience upon learning he or she had a terminal illness. These stages are: 1) denial and isolation, 2) anger, 3) bargaining, 4) depression and 5) acceptance. This book focused more on the person who is dying as opposed to the person who lost a loved one; later, the stages were used to describe a bereaved individual's grieving process.

Kubler-Ross's final book co-authored with David Kessler, in 1974, was written while she was dying and published afterwards. This book re-introduces the "Five stages of Grief" as a framework to apply our learning from mourning. These grief stages are unique and universal to anyone. It is applicable to individuals who are mourning in response to their own terminal illness, the loss of a loved one, or even the death of a pet. Not everyone goes through these stages in a specific order. We can move between stages. Some people do not go through every one of these stages. It is a grieving process and tools to help individuals identify what they are feeling. Understanding these stages of grief may help better guide us through coping with life and our loss.

As we are able to look at how mourning feels, and how it affects our lives and the lives of those around us we can begin the healing process. While it is important in understanding the possible stages and symptoms of grieving, it does not take away the pain of the loss we may experience. "The five stages—denial, anger, bargaining, depression, and acceptance—are a part of the framework that makes up our learning to live with the one we lost."[10]

Stage I: Denial / Shock

Shock and disbelief accompany the denial stage. "You begin to question the how and why. How did this happen? You may ask, as you review the circumstances."[11] You may say to yourself, "Its okay, this is not happening to me." This first stage of grieving helps us to survive the loss. As you begin to ask yourself questions, this is the beginning of the healing process.

When death is unexpected and sudden, you may feel cheated. There has been no time for preparation, no time to say good-bye. You had no opportunity to prepare for it in any way. Moreover, when the death is also traumatic, accompanied by other complicating circumstance such as violence or mass destruction, an overwhelming sense of shock and disbelief may settle in. "It can't be!" These feelings may occur even when death is expected. The reality of the actual death may still be overwhelming for some individuals

Stage II: Anger

The anger grief stage usually occurs when we feel helpless. We may ask, "How can this be happening to me? Who is to blame?" There may be a sense of unfairness. This stage is critical because the anger may become displaced if not properly released. Venting anger can be done constructively or destructively. Hitting a doll is much preferred than striking a person. Individuals may turn to chemicals and alcohol for temporary relief. Alcohol is a depressant and the grief process is already depressing. Self-medicating should be avoided and it can be extremely dangerous. You may want to consult a physician before self-medicating to relieve stress. A physician may prescribe medication to alleviate anxiety and stress. You should follow the instructions of the prescriptions and report any changes in symptoms to your physician.

Therapist and counselors responsibility is to be good listeners and monitor changes in behaviors in their clients. Therapist need to have a clear understanding of their clients' strengths and limitations so they can appropriately assist them. Therapist/Counselors need to use discretion when dealing with clients who display behaviors that are out of the scope of their practice to handle. Adequate referrals to other professionals to further assist their clients, should be done when needed.

The relaxation response is a helpful way to cope with anger. It is a natural way to turn off the fight or flight response and bring the body back to pre-stress levels. Steps to elicit relaxation response is a healing tool that one can achieve for themselves. Adding an exercise such as the one shown at the following website, http://www.relaxationresponse.org/steps/, can help reduce stress.

Stage III: Bargaining

The bargaining stage gives us a sense of hope that if we can negotiate for more time with our loved one. We make this negotiation with God or a higher power we believe in for an exchange to "get it right", with others and ourselves. In this stage, we may feel and say, "I'll change my lifestyle for more time"; I'll do whatever I need to do for my time to see my grandchild be born".

"Guilt is often bargaining's companion. The "if only" mindset causes us to find fault with ourselves and what we "think" we could have done differently. We may even bargain with the pain. We will do anything not to feel the pain of this loss. We remain in the past, trying to negotiate our way out of the hurt".[12]

Most clients I have met with have expressed some form of grief. Their guilt was expressed out of unresolved conflicts with their loved ones. Thinking you could have prevented the death of a loved one can contribute to guilt feelings.

Losing a child, whether it be from an accident or illness, often leave parents feeling how they could have changed things to prevent the death. Sometimes they wonder if they did something wrong in their own lives or in raising the child, to cause the death.

In counseling, people who have lost their parents after placing them in a nursing home. I have found that some of these clients have thoughts of ever removing their parent from the home. Additionally, because the loss is something they feel they could have controlled, like keeping their parent at home nearby so they could have monitored their care more closely. They lose sight of their sound reasons of their decision of a proper placement of their parent.

Sudden unexpected deaths of a loved one can create a sense of guilt related to feelings lack of control over the death. Especially, violent deaths of a loved one brings about many questions about the crime that are often unanswered. Again, assuming the blame, family and close friends may feel as though they have failed the deceased. Though, questions of "why didn't I play closer attention" or why didn't I see the signs of trouble", can contribute to feelings of self-blame.

Suicide deaths may leave loved ones with the guilt of believing there must have been something they could have done to prevent the death. However, it is important for them to understand that the individual made a choice to end their life and you had no control over their decision.

Bargaining with God or higher power may be helpful in allowing us to ultimately rely on that Supreme Being. We then can take control over the situation and our lives. Overall, individuals need to be reminded they are not responsible for the deaths of their loved ones. Should we develop unresolved issues with blame and guilt, it may lead to depression.

Stage IV: Depression

Depression often is described as feeling sad, blue, irritable, emptiness, unhappy, and at times fearful. Some of us experience these symptoms at one point or another during our lives for a short period, depending on what precipitated these symptoms. These feelings may present themselves during different stages of grief. Suffering a major loss like the death of a loved one can knock you off your feet for a period of time. However, you still maintain your self-esteem and emotional connections with family and friends. It is natural to feel sadness, uncertainty and reflect on the relationship you had with your love one. Sometimes people may feel, "I am so down, why do anything." The lack of interest in usual activities may present itself.

Kubler-Ross and Kessler wrote, " ...in grief, depression is a way for nature to keep us protected by shutting down the nervous system so that we can adapt to something we feel we cannot handle."[13]

However, individuals need time to express their sad feelings of loss they have experienced. It shows that they have started the process of greater acceptance of the reality of the death. When we allow ourselves to release these emotions, we are then engaging in the healing process. Most people will eventually show signs of resiliency and return to relatively normal functioning.

When monitoring the depressed state of the bereaved, we should keep in mind the difference of symptoms of the normal reactions to loss and sadness. In serious depression, it is constant and intractable. In bereavement, it is intermittent and comes in "waves". The grieving person may feel like they will return to the way they used to do things, unlike the seriously depressed individual, who may feel they want to join the deceased, or even suicidal.

When clinical depression is observed in an individual, an appropriate professional referral is then required for further management of the symptoms.

Stage V: Acceptance

This fifth stage we begin to recognize some peace with the reality of the death. Depending on the individual, there are enhanced degrees of acceptance, and reduced grief. Complete acceptance of death may not be a realistic goal. The acceptance to which Kubler-Ross refers is a state of emotional acceptance of our loss. "This stage is about accepting the reality that our loved one is physically gone and recognizing that this new reality is the permanent reality. We will never like this reality or make it acceptable, but eventually we accept it".[14]

The acceptance stage allows us to reshape and plan our lives in a way that honors our loss and not be constantly consumed by it. We can begin to make adjustments in our lives. To promote healing, we learn how to live productively without our loved one. Memorable experiences we shared with our loved ones remain in our thoughts. We move towards integrating our loss into our lives that will help us to move forward in a healthy way.

Even though the grief experience is often characterized by phases or stages, Kubler –Ross reminds us, "Grief is not just a series of events, stages, or timeliness."[15] There is no correct way to grieve, and there is no way to anticipate exactly how the feelings of emptiness, sadness, loneliness, anger and resentment will heal.

Carol Staudacher (1991) divided the grieving process into three major phases: retreating, working through and resolving. Retreating happens immediately after the death of a loved one as a way of temporarily managing pain and anxiety. Common experiences and feelings during this phase are shock, numbness, disbelief, confusion, disorientation and denial.

Working through is the next phase, during which a mourner confronts, endures and works through various grief responses, including sadness, confusion, despair, feelings of abandonment, powerless, loss of control, helplessness, specific and unspecific fear, anger, guilt, auditory or visual hallucinations, depression, and poor concentration and memory. Working through these responses helps the mourner enter the resolving phase, during which mourners restructure their lives to adjust to an environment of which the loved one is no longer a part.

Anticipatory Grief

Anticipatory grief occurs before the death of a loved one occurs. Anticipatory grief is a common grief reaction of individuals who are facing the impending death of their loved ones. It is different from grief that follows death, but it may carry many of the symptoms of regular grief such as anxiety, sadness, isolation and fear. This kind of grief is not often discussed or some individuals find it socially unacceptable to express this type of grief they are experiencing. As a result, this type of grief can lead to unresolved issues about grieving and lack of support.

Complicated Grief

Complicated grief refers to a persistent form of bereavement that is overwhelming and controls an individual's life. It interferes with daily living functions for an extended period. Suppression of the grief process denies individuals the opportunity to express their pain or respond to the realities of what happened and can be traumatic and subsequently cause death. This is not considered healthy grieving and it warrants professional intervention to assist individuals with effective coping skills.

Ira J. Tanner explains grief morbidity, "Grief slips into morbidity when we grow preoccupied with thoughts of suicide or talk of nothing other than the loss."[16]

Often it can be very difficult for individuals to share their grief with others. Thoughts of how others will perceive how they are coping with their loss may preoccupy their mind, as well as thoughts of others not being able to grasp the understanding of how you are feeling. Another barrier of sharing grief may stem from ownership of our grief, "my grief is my grief, and it belongs to me."

Tanner further sheds light on the significance of sharing our loss:

> Upon losing someone or something important to us, we need to talk Immediately of the how, when, and where aspects of the loss. Our minds are foggy after loss. The loss may have occurred before our eyes, but until someone asks us a few pointed questions requiring us to sort the facts, those facts are not clear to us.[17]

Special help is needed when symptoms become so intense and severe; it causes risks to our physical, emotional, or spiritual well-being. It is vital that we get extra support. Church affiliations are a good source of support, along with peer support groups, counseling, therapist, and psychologist. A psychiatrist may also be beneficial in exploring coping strategies. Seeking support from those who specializes in loss and grief can be more helpful in meeting your needs.

This type of grief is also described as the pain that does not go away. There are some experts that argue that complicated grief or prolonged grief disorder should not be considered a separate condition in the DSM-IV manual (the American Psychiatric Association's Guide for Diagnosing Mental Disorders). Currently, there is no formal definition of complicated grief. However, when grief persists, it interferes with your daily activities of life and your preoccupation for desiring the presence of your loved one makes you unable to express any form of contentment in your life. Complicated grieving can smother your sense of reality and your coping abilities.

Emotional pain may lead to feelings of heat-break or loneliness, often leaving you to question if you are going to be all right. The anxiety from the pain is so great; it leaves you pondering how you will survive it. Freedom from emotional pain comes along with assurance that you will no longer be afraid of feeling emotional pain, or even that you can tolerate the pain.

To heal emotional pain, we need to bring it to the forefront of our conscious awareness and spend time with ourselves. As we do this, we may find an infinite source of well-being that is always available to us from within. We will then be able to exhale.

Methods of adjusting to emotional pain may include prayer, meditation, family support, community support, church support, support groups, and counseling.

CHAPTER 4

The Pain of Grief

When we think of death, loss, grieving and bereavement, we come to the realization that it is time to say our final good-bye. It is a challenge to face because it is painful. In addition to the hurting, we feel all sorts of emotions associated with the idea of death; we may feel anxiety, despair, and confusion. Sometimes we experience mixed emotions. There can be relief experienced when death finally comes from long-term illnesses, often followed by guilt for feeling relieved. We hurt even though we know their suffering is gone. This can be very exhausting because the process of grief takes energy.

Some aspects of death, pain and suffering is to seek a deeper understanding and meaning of it. David Baker further adds that one should consider the book of Job as a literary approach to understanding the meaning of pain, sacrifice and suffering:

> Pain is the common companion of birth and growth, disease and death, and is phenomenon deeply intertwined with the very question of human existence ... To attempt to understand the nature of pain, to seek to find its meaning, is already to respond to an imperative of pain itself. No experience demands and insists upon interpretation in the same way. Pain forces the question

> of its meaning and especially of its cause insofar as cause
> is an important part of its meaning.[18]

The recent death of my ex-husband (October 2014), the father of our physically and intellectually challenged son, forced me into a state of mourning, not just for myself but also for our son. Though our son has the ability to understand and reason life experiences to some degree, his cognitive functioning is limited. Our son had recently spent time with his father. Thomas, (not his real name) and I expected the death of his father. We had time to say good-bye.

I endured the pain of telling Thomas his father had "passed away" and that was not an easy task since I had to explain his dad's death in a way in which he could understand it. Because his father's heritage is from West Africa, the head of their family requested Thomas to write a tribute for his father. After carefully listening to Thomas' interpretation of death, we wrote the tribute, and forwarded to the "head of the family".

Now that Thomas' father is gone, the pain is so big. Thomas has many questions about what will happen in his life. He asked, "When will I see him again? Is that why I don't get my checks in the mail? How are we going to make it?" Some of Thomas' questions I can attempt to answer, some I cannot at this time. Thomas' suffering is my suffering. I trust in the Holy Spirit for guidance.

The difficult experience of losing a loved one is often unexplainable with pain so indescribable. C.S. Lewis describes a common reaction; "But there are other difficulties. "Where is she now?" That is, in what place is she now?"[19]

Death is irreversible and all living things must die. Death is looked at, as final. Often we find ourselves with the pain of not being able to understand it. "You can't see anything properly while your eyes are blurred with tears. You can't, in most things, get what you want if you want it too desperately: anyway, you can't get the best out of it. "Now!"[20]

As we embark on the mourning, we want to be pain free, and often we want it now. However, it will take a process for the pain to be less heightened. After all, it hurts, and the hurt is real.

Tragic deaths can cause immense pain because usually they occur without notice. Jerry Sittser describes this type of experience as "Sudden and tragic loss that leads to terrible darkness. It is as inescapable as nightmares during a high fever. The darkness comes no matter how hard we try to hold it off. However threating, we must face it and we must face it alone."[21]

Facing the death experience alone hurts. How do you share your hurts? Do you really want to share your hurt? These questions may enter into one's mind, as we are hurting. People may face a myriad of issues in their thought process during their pain. "Deep sorrow often has the effect of stripping life of pretense, vanity, and waste. It forces us to ask basic questions about what is most important in life."[22]

Individuals will need to apply tools to ease their pain and suffering. "Unforgiveness does not stop the pain."[23]

Forgiveness appears in various forms. The act of forgiveness is dependent on reasons why to forgive, whether it is forgiving yourself or your deceased loved one for real or perceived events that have occurred. "The process of forgiveness begins when the victim realizes that nothing, not justice or revenge or anything else, can reverse the wrong done. Forgiveness cannot spare victims the consequences of loss, nor can it recover the life they once had."[24]

Forgiveness allows us to release negative energy and replace our thoughts with positive energy. Forgiveness allows us to move forward by releasing the pain and welcoming peace in our lives. "However difficult, forgiveness in the end brings freedom to the one who gives it."[25] Forgiveness is a key to healing. God gives us His grace and mercy daily. This act of love by God demonstrates to us His forgiving nature. "Forgiving people, therefore, define the role they play in life modestly. They simply let God be God so they can be normal and happy human beings who learn to forgive."[26]

Dealing with Grief and Loss during Holidays

Holidays, birthdays, anniversaries and other special times shared with the deceased can be very stressful events without your loved ones. The loss of a loved one can hurt more on these special occasions. This can be difficult and each person deals with it differently. Special events intensify grief because they focus feelings of loss. The absence of your loved one will alter or completely change the traditions you shared, which in turn may cause you to relive many memorable experiences.

In addition to heightened grief, you may also experience other emotions such as apprehension of the pain that will color former celebrations, or anxiety about related preparations. It is normal to experience a strong desire to avoid the entire event. You may feel uncertain because you do not know what to do and you think that your plans are not right without your loved one.

Approaching Traditions

Acknowledging that special days will be different is the first step to approaching these events. Keep in mind that for most, the anticipation of special days are usually worse than the actual experience. You may want to treat the holidays or special days the same way as you do other important days. When planning for special days, reflect on experiences. Memories of what was enjoyable are healthy. Allow yourself to feel sad because the person is no longer with you.

It is acceptable to enjoy yourself. You may need to modify some traditions, particularly if your loved one played a strong role. Communicate with other family members and expect that feelings of grief will be shared and supported by each other.

You may find that some traditions are no longer applicable. Whether you pursue older or newer traditions, you can still include your loved one. Hanging their favorite ornament on the tree, preparing their favorite dish, or including a photo at events are ways that everyone can honor in sharing memories. This can be comforting and may allow family and friends to reaffirm their feelings about the one who is no longer present.

CHAPTER 5

What The Bible Says About Grieving

Religious organizations historically have provided a safe environment for its members and others to help people deal with their issues surrounding grief and bereavement. Churches and other religious groups have cared for the sick or the dying, the burial or disposal of the dead and supported the bereaved and their family. Geoff Walter noted that not much has been written from as theological perspective about these significant activities:

> I noticed that most helpful wisdom on the subject of bereavement was coming from secular, usually psychological, sources. Christian books, with a few notable exceptions seemed either to repeat the pronouncements of the psychologist with little or no theological critique or to avoid the real issues facing the bereaved people by flight into the next world.[27]

Walter shares that lack of literature on bereavement following the death of loved ones has made many Christians embarrassed or created a drawback as they measured their responses to loss against uninformed faith. The task of the next paragraph is to explore how bible traditions have unveiled the process of grief among males in their response to the loss of their loved ones.

Expression of Grief

The pain and suffering of separation remains in the heart of many individuals who lose their loved ones. The scars and the void of loss are real for as long as we live or until we also meet our maker. Consequently, various groups of people have designed ways that helps them to cope with their losses. "In the Old Testament, the grieving process is described as fulfilling a legal and cultural necessity, rather than being an expression of personal grief."[28] It can be argued therefore that cultural practices of grief may at times address grief in a formalized way without giving particular attentions to the individual's emotional and psychological content. Exemplifying the experience of elderly partners in bereavement Walter affirms that:

1. There is an acute expression of grief in private whereas dignity is maintained in the public manifestation.
2. There is a concern to "do things properly in terms of the rites of disposal."
3. There is a desire to do the best for the oved one even beyond death.
4. There is an acknowledged psychological need for a place of remembrance (Genesis 37:31-35, I Samuel 15:11).

The assumption by Walter that cultural practices in grief addresses grief in a formalized way without giving particular individuals emotional and psychological content, may have ignored the fact that mourning ceremonies in other cultures allows the bereaved to vent out their grief in a formalized way while focusing and befitting the bereaving individuals in a community. The bereaved may be restored from their shock and sorrow to a normal status; and their relations with the dead is established since relationships continue beyond death.

Males and Grief in the Old Testament

Upon receiving the news of the loss of their sons, shock overcame both Jacob and David, as well as Job regarding the loss of his sons and daughters. Their exclamations were of great psychological truth and shocking effect to them. Jacob's mourning of his son lingered; "Then Jacob tore his clothes, put on sackcloth and mourned for his son many days. All his sons and daughters came to comfort him, but he refused to be comforted. 'No,' he said, 'in mourning will I go down to the grave to my son.' So his father wept for him." (Genesis 37:34-35) Jacob is showing the visible signs of mourning and he is showing that he may come to terms with the loss but his mourning would not end because of the impact of his loss. This demonstrates that the amount of love we invest in a person relates to how much pain we suffer because of their death. Individuals who have lost their loved ones find it difficult to completely cope with their loss, especially the loss of children. When they witness their friends and family making some progress with funeral preparations for example, buying a dress or a suit for their parent's funeral or buying the casket, the pain comes back.

Another narrative is that of David's expression of grief following the death of Saul's son, Jonathan. When he received the news of the death of Saul and Jonathan, David was both shocked and inquisitive. He asked, "What happened? How do you know that Saul and his son Jonathan are dead?" (2Samuel 1:4-5). This according to Kubler-Ross and other contemporary theorist is a normal reaction to this sudden bereavement, and here we see the shock, disbelief and an anxious need to verify the facts. "Then David and all the men with him took hold of their clothes and tore them. They mourned and wept and fasted til evening for Saul and his son Jonathan, and for the army of the LORD and the house of Israel, because they had fallen by the sword." (2 Samuel 1: 11-12). After the expression of shock and anger, David's grief extended from expression of personal grief to sharing of national feeling by killing the messenger. We often let our emotions control us and we selfishly turn to them for comfort instead of trusting God in the situation we face. David, a man after God's own heart and God's chosen one, like Jacob whom we have already observed, faced grief in full pain without any attempt to find consolation in the grace of God.

Account of David's grief recorded

1. Shock/disbelief on learning of the news of death.
2. An expression of grief, once the news of death had been shared.
3. Violent blame of those present at the death and held responsible.
4. Distressed visualization of the scene of death.
5. Glorified praise of the deceased.
6. An outpouring of intimate, personal feelings.
7. Refusal to find comfort even in admirable beliefs.

When David received the news about the death of his son Absalom, David was overcome with the news. He retreated into his private room and cried, "O my son Absalom! My son, my son, Absalom! If only I had died instead of you – O Absalom, my son, my son!" (2 Samuel 18:33). Though David understood it was not possible to retain both the throne and his son, he was still overcome by grief.

Yet another narrative is that of Job's expression of grief following the news about the death of his daughters and sons, "Your sons and daughters were feasting and drinking wine at the oldest brother's house, when suddenly a mighty wind swept in from the desert and struck the four corners of the house. It collapsed on them and they are dead." (Job 1:18-19) The impact of the loss was so great for Job, yet he continued to worship the Lord. His outward expression of his lost was shown to all. "At this, Job got up and tore his robe and shaved his head. Then he fell to the ground in worship and said, "Naked I came from my mother's womb, and naked I will depart. The LORD gave and the LORD has taketh away; may the name of the LORD be praised." (Job 1: 20-21)

The implication of this is that Job, during all of his grieving, continued to trust in the Lord. This illustration is a comfort to those who feel despaired at the loss of a loved one. The realization that our trust lies with God, is consoling within itself.

Walter asserts that:

1. In all the stories written by a variety of authors at different times and in different political and religious contexts, the reality of grief is fully acknowledged. The need to grieve should not be restricted.
2. It has been traditional among biblical scholars to account for differences in detail of the narratives in terms of textual theories. However, these differences may be attributed to differences in the circumstances and personalities of the protagonist.
3. It is startling to discover that, although the people concerned are otherwise depicted by authors as having great religious sensibilities, at no time are their religious beliefs or personal faith in God seen as modifying or even bringing comfort in the experience of grief.

Walters further asserts that these considerations should give light to the experience of Christians today.

Males and Grief in the New Testament

Grief in the New Testament reveals Jesus with a human body, emotions, mind, and will. In addition to possessing a divine nature, the Word became flesh. He became a human. He displayed all the attributes of Humans with the exception of sin (John 1:14). In the Old Testament, Isaiah prophetically tells of Jesus as "a man of sorrows, and familiar with suffering" (Isaiah 53:3). Throughout the Gospels, Jesus displayed human emotions. Jesus demonstrated it is not wrong to grieve.

The Bible clearly reveals that Jesus wept on three occasions; He wept for friends (John 11:35); He wept over his enemies (Luke 19:41), He wept for himself (Hebrews 5:7).

Lazarus, the brother of Mary and Martha of Bethany, were all good friends of Jesus. When Jesus heard, "Lord, the one you love is sick" (John 11:3), He grieved. Jesus comforted the sisters when He learned of the death of their brother. We often comfort one another during our grief of the loss of our loved ones. "Jesus, once more deeply moved, came to the tomb" John 11:38) He then raises Lazarus from the dead. Jesus also expressed being glad that his followers had the opportunity to see Lazarus raised from the dead so their faith would be increased (John 11:15).

What is of interest here is to note Jesus' emotions in John 11. Jesus is shown as both glad and sad regarding the same event. Grief often can be transformed into hopefulness!

Jesus began speaking about who He is, "I am the resurrection and the life. He who believes in me will live, even though he dies; and whoever lives and believes in me will never die." (John 11:25-26) This shows how denial is obvious when one loses a loved one. Jesus spoke of the future to the bereaved. He did not address the current situation in which the bereaved were experiencing. An example of how males would sometimes conveniently want to divert the reality of loss upon receiving the news of the death of a loved one is shown in verse 25. As Jesus witnessed that their situation would not easily accommodate the life after death message, He came to the level of the bereaved and grieved with them, as He too was troubled in his spirit.

The Gospels describe how the disciples' reacted to the crucifixion of Jesus with grief. Luke, the physician, gives us a detailed picture of two people in grief on their way to Emmaus (Luke 24: 13-27), and how men buried and mourned the death of Stephen (Acts 8:2). Above all, grief is a normal response to loss, even for those who hope for resurrection beyond death.

Grieving Women in the Bible

There are many stories of women in the Bible who endured difficult times and suffered losses of their loved ones. Here I will list an example of three other remarkable women in the Bible who courageously and gracefully endured the pain and suffering of death of their loved ones.

Naomi and Ruth's Grief (Old Testament)

Naomi became one of the widows whom Paul described as being "desolate." In addition to her desolation and grief, she also lost both of her sons and so Naomi "was left of her two sons and husband." Her grief was real. Her suffering was long-term until her old age. She was left a beggar in a foreign country. Instead of sinking in her grief with depression or thoughts of suicide, she extended her love and kindness to her daughter-in-law's. Since these two women were kind to Naomi and they also loss their husbands, Naomi asked the Lord to bless them.

Family relationships change due to grief experiences. Ruth, one of Naomi's daughter-in-law's, chose to stay with her during such a time of despair. Her devotion and servitude to her mother-in-law was remarkable. Even in afflictions, death and famine in the land, Naomi and Ruth let love abound. Ruth said to her mother-in-law, "Where you go I will go, and where you stay I will stay. Your people will be my people and your God my God." (Ruth 1:16)

The love these two women shared with each other increased their faith in God. Often times we lose our faith because the one we lost was our protector and our provider. We must always rely on our blessings from the Lord, whatever our situation is.

These women expressed "agape" kind of love. It is the selfless kind of love that seeks the other's best interest:

> Love is patient, love is kind, it does not envy, it does not boast, it is not Proud. It is not rude, it is not self-seeking, it is not easily angered, it keeps no record of wrongs. Love does not delight in evil but rejoices with the truth. It always protects, always trust, always hopes, always preserves. Love never fails. (1Corinthians 13:4-8)

It is easy for many of us to dismiss the real significance of this passage on love because we use the word "love" in so many different ways. For example, "I love cookies," "I love my cat," or "I love my spouse." Too often, our use of the word "love" expresses our feelings. However, the love described in 1 Corinthians 13 is different.

The love Naomi and Ruth had for each other allowed these two mourning widows to understand their love was entwined with grief, but they were overcome with love and kindness during their journey in life.

Naomi and Ruth's loss eventually led to the biggest blessing to humanity. According to the genealogy of Jesus, Boaz marries Ruth, she bears him a son, Obed, whom he is the father of Jessie, whom he is the father of David. Our Savior is a descendent of King David according to Mathew of the Gospels. Mathew begins by calling Jesus the son of David, in which son means descendant, calling to mind the promises God made to David and Abraham (Mathew 1:1). Abraham would be the father of many nations, along with other promises. Jesus will be the true son of God, sit on the throne of David, reign over a never–ending Kingdom, and inherit the land promised to Abraham forever.

The women near the cross who grieved, including Jesus Mother (New Testament)

Nothing prepares you for being present at the death of a loved one. The emotional trauma of the experience can leave you with manifestations of grief. The women near the cross-witnessed the homicide of Jesus. This crucifixion was violent. This experience often shakes the witnesses' sense of safety, control, and trust in the world around them:

> Near the cross of Jesus stood his mother, his mother's sister, Mary the wife of Clopas, and Mary of Magdala. When Jesus saw his mother there, and the disciple whom he loved standing nearby, he said to his mother, "Dear woman, here is your son," and to the disciple, "Here is your mother." From that time on, this disciple took her into his home. (John 19:25)

Jesus mother, Mary, no doubt was experiencing intense emotional reactions. While experiencing the shock and sadness, she also must have felt great relief with the assurance of being cared for by John, the disciple. Grief is often complicated by the uncertainty of the bereaved not knowing of their future provisions.

Jesus mother, brothers, and sisters, along with His disciples and other followers, gathered in the upper room and were instructed by Jesus before His death to wait upon the Holy Spirit to be endued with power to carry on His ministry. "They all joined together constantly in prayer, along with the women and Mary the mother of Jesus, and his brothers." (Acts1:14) This scripture depicts Jesus mother utilizing a powerful tool- prayer, which is commanded by God for all us. "Be joyful always; pray continuously; give thanks in all circumstances, for this is God's will for you in Christ Jesus" (1Thessalonians 16-18)

Interesting enough that Jesus mother is never mentioned again in the scriptures. Her example of praying brought us power through the Holy Spirit of God. This sort of power is not exclusive to any one person.

The Holy Spirit gives us power to do what is impossible without Him. Used in the right way, this power will bring glory to God and blessings to your life as well as others. Prayer is the only thing no one religion can claim possession of or origination of. It is not denominational or a religious experience. Prayer is an individual experience that takes place between the Creator and those whom He created."[29] The power of prayer can help us overcome our grief.

CHAPTER 6

Counseling and Grief Support

The Christian counselor has the ability to look to God to solve problems and we look to Scriptures to reveal truth and direction. The counselor can offer spiritual direction to the bereaved. Mark R. McMinn asserts, "Though less important than a client's relationship with God, the counseling relationship is more often a mechanism by which God's grace is introduced to a hurting person. By fostering a healthy Christian-counseling relationship, with or without the explicit use of Scripture, we provide clients with a glimpse of God's grace."[30]

Christians believe that the Bible contains the very words and presence of God. They are His words to us. McMinn suggest that the power of Scripture transforms lives; "It is powerful, active, and useful for training ourselves to be righteous."[31] The Bible offers benefits to clinical work. It offers reassurance, instruction, and comfort. Counselors want to provide comfort to counselees. The Scriptures add value to counseling; it exists to connect us to God.

The effectiveness of using prayer in Professional Counseling may be challenging. McMinn explains that it is crucial for counselors to evaluate their personal prayer patterns before introducing prayer into counseling sessions. "Spiritually transforming prayer takes time and disciplined training. For prayer to be an active agent for change in a client's life, it must become part of a disciplined spiritual life outside the counseling office."[32] The bereaved will need to practice praying to help them draw closer to God and seek comfort.

When it comes to using prayer in counseling, one ethical concern is that counselors must never push their own beliefs or values on their clients. Prayer should be used in counseling only if the client desires it. When counselors pray before a counseling session, it helps to seek wisdom and peace from God.

To ascertain that there is no misunderstanding between counselor and counselee about spiritual interventions used, McMinn further asserts:

> The best solution to this problem is to describe the nature of counseling in a written informed-consent form that is reviewed and signed by the client before beginning treatment. The consent form will be different for each client and should include a discussion of spiritual interventions that might be used for treatment.[33]

Fostering a clear understanding of the purpose and use of Scripture in counseling also promotes ethical standards. Utilizing informed consent, using discretion of when charging fees and filing insurance claims for scriptural use in counseling avoids the risk of non-payment for services. In addition, grieving people are sometimes shadowed by their grief that their minds may not be as astute as it normally would be. The Christian Counselor's primary responsibility is to protect the client's best interest.

Exercise, Rest, Meditation and Healthy Eating Can Help the Grieving Process

Exercise:

There are psychological and physiological benefits of exercise. Physical activity is therapeutic for your mind. When you exercise, it requires focus while providing you a sense of control. Its impact on your brain increases blood flow to that organ of the body, allowing it to almost immediately function better. The psychological benefits of exercise promote positive thinking and improved mood and clarity of thoughts.

Endorphins are chemicals that pass messages to the brain when stimulated. Its role is to promote that 'feel good factor.' Exercise is a known activity that stimulates the production of endorphins in the body.

Serotonin is another chemical in the body that is associated with brain activity and mood. This neurotransmitter is also linked to depression. Exercise helps regulate serotonin levels in the brain, which lessons anxiety and improves one's overall wellbeing.

Walking can be a great exercise. This low-impact exercise has many health benefits. One can choose to walk a pet, walk around the block, walk to a corner store, or even walk in the mall. One can get involved while having fun with recreational activities like hiking, skating, bike riding, bowling, dancing, or gardening. Take a walk while on the cell phone; use the stairs instead of the elevator at work or church. A pedometer is a device that can help to count the number of steps a person takes throughout the day and help increase the number taken each week. One can also participate at their local health club. It may feel motivating to join others in a setting that promotes physical health benefits.

Rest and Meditation

Rest and sleep is another important health issue. Adequate rest and sleep can help the bereaved cope better with their loss. Mathew Edlund expounds on the four kinds of active rest the body needs:

> **Mental rest** means focusing intelligently on your environment in a way that's rejuvenating. Techniques of mental rest give you the ability to obtain calm and relaxed

concentration quickly and effectively and to become relaxed and focused anytime and anywhere. **Social rest** means using the power of social connectedness to relax and rejuvenate. Your walk to lunch with your colleague is a small example of social rest. **Spiritual rest** is the practice of connecting with things larger and greater than ourselves, which provides fellowship and meaning in life-factors people hunger for like food. Spiritual rest can create a sense of internal balance and personal security while proving comfort where none appears to exist. **Physical rest,** by focusing your body and its simplest physiological processes, provokes calm, relaxation, mental alertness, and surprisingly better health.[34]

The goal of meditation is to focus and quiet your mind, reaching a higher level of awareness and inner calm. Meditation is completely free! It requires no special equipment. It can be practiced anywhere, anytime (10-15 minutes per day is good). There are no health side effects of meditation.

Healthy Eating

Generally people seem to know what foods are healthy – fruits, vegetables, chicken, fish, lean meat, whole grain breads, brown rice, skim milk or 1% milk, etc. Avoiding fried foods, baked and broiled foods are healthier. Portion control is vital to our health. Small portions for breakfast, lunch and dinner, with a snack in the morning and afternoon are much healthier than larger meals.

Food can change your mood. People who are grieving sometimes lose their appetite because of their grief stricken state. However, they need to be encouraged to consume a healthy diet to nourish their brain and their body. Eating more fish is beneficial to a good state of mind. Mounting evidence says that Omega-3 fatty acids (found abundantly in fatty fish such as salmon, herring, sardines, and tuna) may help depressive symptoms. However, if one is allergic to seafood, they should avoid fish.

Water is your body's principal chemical component and makes up about 60 percent of your body weight. Lack of water can lead to dehydration, a condition that occurs when you do not have enough water in your body to carry out normal functions. Water also carries nutrients to your cells.

It is widely recommended to drink eight, 8-ounce glasses that equals about 2 liters or a half gallon a day. This is called the 8x8 rule. This rule is not supported by hard evidence but it remains popular because it is easy to remember. However, the Institute of Medicine recommends that men should roughly drink 13 cups (3liters) of beverages per day. Women should drink about 9 cups (2.2) liters) of beverage a day.

First Lady Michelle Obama has made it readily available for Americans to remember what a healthy diet looks like — the government has recently released images of her Nutrition Plate. The plate is divided into four sections, for fruit, vegetables, grains and protein- a smaller circle sits beside the plate. For dairy products, choose MyPlate.gov.

Oftentimes food, water and beverages are brought to the house of the bereaved by other family members, friends, community, and church members.

Food is served after the celebration of life services. Other than nourishment for the body, food is also used while communicating, socializing and uplifting one another.

The Power of Human Connections

Some mourning is best done in private, but seek help from others when you need to do so. Your friends and family members may not know how to help you or may be afraid of the intensity and duration of your grief. Sometimes in their helplessness, they may withdraw from you. Stay connected with the survivors. There is a healing power in knowing that no one is alone. When you feel loved, nurtured, cared for, supported and intimate, you are much likely to be happier and healthier.

Support Network

Social support is a key instrument for helping people handle stressful situations. A social support network is comprised of family, friends and peers who provide support during stressful situations. This is not the same as a support group that is organized by a mental health professional. Unlike a support group, your social support network is not structured or formalized. You don't have to sit in a group and discuss the stressful times you are enduring. Luncheons, phone calls to family and friends, or texting your siblings, children, or counseling with church ministerial staffs are ways to express your stressful experiences while fortifying your relationships.

Grief Support Groups

These type of groups one can be beneficial should a person feel they require a structured, organized setting to share and grow from their stressful experiences. People who share similar experiences attend these groups. A grief support group is usually led by a mental health professional with grief counseling experience. This type of support includes fighting fears since it is normal to be afraid to confront your losses and all the changes they bring.

Support groups allow individuals to share their hurt and pain with each other. It also offers coping strategies that others in the group have utilized to further assist them with dealing with their loss.

Grief support groups offer companionship and understanding from others who have experienced similar loss and have faced similar challenges that accompany grief.

You are likely to find the following at grief support settings:

- Non-judgmental emotional and physical support.
- An opportunity to begin the healing process by expressing your personal experiences and listening to others share their personal experiences.

- Support and understanding from others in the group.
- Sound coping skills to assist you through your grief process.
- Hope of restoration and healing.
- The opportunity of staying connected with others and exploring creative ways to stay in touch with survivors and others.

For people who want to support the bereaved, it is important to remember that few people are good at expressing and coping with grief. One cannot practice the feelings of loss ahead of time. You do not have to feel inadequate when offering support. Just say what is in your heart and try to be tactful in your approach to the bereaved.

Available Resources

Since we have reviewed the grieving process and the necessity to grieve the loss of loved ones and the creative opportunities for counselors to service the bereaved, I will impart effective resources that I am confident will enthuse, and inspire us to become more effective in grief counseling ministry.

Bereavement Parents of the USA
National Office
Post Office Box 622
St. Peters, MO 63376
800.273.8255
Email: bereavedparentsusa.org

Offers support, especially to parents, grandparents, or siblings struggling to rebuild their lives after loss.

Center for Grief Recovery
1263 West Loyola Avenue
Chicago, IL 60626
773.274.4600
Email: information grief counselor.org

Comprised of Counselors and Psychotherapist who empower people to heal themselves and enrich their lives.

Covenant United Church of Christ
1130 East 154th Street
South Holland, IL 60473
708.333.5955
Fax: 708.333.4220
Website: www.covcc.org
Email: info@covucc.org

This Church offers a Beloved Ministry and Caregiver Support Ministry, which includes training courses to assist and support care providers. The Beloved Ministry also offers follow-up for one year of family members after the loss of their loved one. These ministries help individuals and families to understand that it is possible to get through this difficult time, help is available, and that healing is attainable. These services include anticipatory grief as well.

First United Methodist Church at the Chicago Temple
77 West Washington St
Chicago, IL 60602
312.236.4548 ext.117.
Website: chicagotemple.org

This temple has a bereavement ministry. They offer certified counselors for all people who have recently experienced grief and loss. They are also available for those who seek counseling, for grief and loss that they are still struggling with adjustment and restoration from grief and loss. They provide two meetings a month for grieving individuals, there are counselors/volunteers readily available to assist.

Life Solutions Counseling
645 W. Carmel Dr., Suite 160
Carmel, IN 46032
317.569. LIFE (5433)
Fax: 317.569.1767
Email: infor@lifesolutionspc.com

Counseling practices that provides professional services that will help improve your mind, spirit, and wellness in life.

Mental Health America (MHA) Live Your Life Well
2000 N. Beauregard Street, 6th Floor
Alexandra, VA 22311
703.684.7722

Fax: 703.684.5968
Toll Free 800.969.6642
Website: http://www.liveyourlifewell.org/
Email: www.mentalhealth of America.net

Their website is designed to help you cope better with stress and create a state of well-being and to be better content with your life.

National Alliance for Grieving Children
900 SE Ocean Blvd, Suite 1300
Stuart, FL 34994
866.432.1542

Assist with finding support and resources for grieving children and their families.

National Hospice and Palliative Care Organization
1731 King Street
Alexandria, VA
703.837.1500
Fax: 703.837.1233
Website: www.nhpco.org/

Engages in wide spectrum and specific grief and bereavement issues.

National Institute on Aging
31 Center Drive, MSC 2292
Bethesda, MD 20892
800.222.2225
TTY: 800.222.4225
Email and Website: niaic@nia.nih.gov

This organization commits to understanding the aged population; they support the health and well- being of older adults. They feature many health topics and they offer various resources for older adults.

National Self-Help Clearing House
33 West 42 Street
Room 1337
New York, New York 10036
212.840.1259

This organization consist of self-help groups that that help the bereaved to cope with their loss. This clearinghouse can provide information about groups operating in your area.

National Students of AMF Support Network
3344 Hillsborough Street, Suite 260
Raleigh, NC 27607
919.803.6728
Toll Free: 877.830.7442
Website: studentsofamf.org

This organization is focusses on supporting college students grieving the illness or death of a loved one. They provide programs, which develops achievement of knowledge, skills, and practical skills in defined specialty practices.

The American Academy of Grief Counseling
2400 Niles- Cortland Rd. SE. Suite #4
Warren, Ohio 44484
330.652.7776
Fax: 652.7575
Website: aihcp.org

They offer continued education, for those who practice and promote health care to individuals and their families. The also offer certifications, recertification, and continuing education (CEU) approval courses.

Transcendental Meditation
Meditation Center

1 E Erie St, #250
Chicago, IL 60611
224.735.3191
Website: tm.org

They offer meditation exercises effective to reduce stress and anxiety.

USDA Center for Nutrition and Promotion
3101 Park Center Drive
Alexandria, VA 22302-1594
202.720.4423
Information Hotline: 202.720.2791
Website: ChooseMyPlate.gov

The United States Government offers images of healthy eating which is a life style change to a better nutritious way of living. These images of the Nutrition Plate is available on their website and you may call to receive a free "My Plate." They also have magnets of the "My Plate," which can be placed on your refrigerator. They also offer good information about nutritional subjects. They also provide information on food labeling requirements for restaurants, similar retail food establishments, and vending machine.

Other Information Sources

Local support attained by contacting one or more of the following:

- Your church affiliation
- The pastoral care staff at local hospitals
- Local community information centers
- Local funeral or cemetery directors
- Local Community Mental Health Centers
- Bereavement Support Groups
- Faith Based Organizations

CONCLUSION

We live in a world where terrible things happen to people. Death can present itself through accidents, act of nature (Hurricane Katrina, New Orleans), homicide, suicide, sickness, and natural causes. Whatever the reason, we normally cry out when we are hurt. We wonder, Why me?

Even Jesus had a similar question when He was here on earth "My God, my God," He cried out as He hung on the cross, "'why have you forsaken me?" (Mark 15:34).

The answers to such questions is totally in God's hands and God alone. We must remember, however, that in the end, the power of miracles—and the reasons for them—remain in God's hands. We must trust that God knows the answers, even if we do not, and that we will not know until we can ask Him face to face in heaven.

Jesus did not practice suppression of grief. He demonstrated grief. Anticipatory grief and grief that follows the loss of a loved one should be expressed to enable the healing process.

Expression of grief depends on numerous factors, which range from emotional and physical closeness of the family, how the family views grief, their role, and relationship to their deceased love one, the individual's spiritual, psychosocial status and whether or not there are available support systems. Since grief is universal and timeless, the process can be more endurable as we rely on our Christian faith to get through this difficult time. We must remember we do not need permission to grieve.

END NOTES

[1] Wikipedia contributors, "Human bonding," Wikipedia, The Free Encyclopedia, http://en.wikipedia.org/windex.php?title=Human_bonding&oldid=623411165 (accessed September 10, 2014).

[2] Bob Deits, Life after Loss: A Practical Guide to Renewing Your Life after Experiencing Major Loss, 5th ed. (Ambridge, Ma: De Capo Press, 2009), 9.

[3] H. Norman Wright, Experiencing Grief (Nashville, TN: BEtH Publishing Group, 2004), 5.

[4] Janice Harris Lord, "Grief and Loss", Family Caregiver Alliance Journal (December 17, 2012), 3.

[5] Frank A. Jones, The Inconvenient Truths of God (Oakland, CA: Word of Truths Publications, 2006), 128.

[6] Ibid. 130.

[7] Archibald D. Hart, Adrenaline, and Stress, (Dallas, London, Vancouver, Melbourne: WORD PUBLISHING, 1995), 7.

[8] Ibid. 11.

[9] Elisabeth Kubler-Ross and David Kessler, ON GRIEF and GRIEVING, (New York, NY: SCRIBNER, 2005), 203.

[10] Ibid., 7.

[11] Ibid., 10.

[12] Ibid., 17.

[13] Ibid., 21.

[14] Ibid., 24, 25.

[15] Ibid., 203.

[16] Irene J Tanner, The Gift of Grief (New York, New York: Hawthorn Books, Inc. 1976), 98.

[17] Ibid., 99.

[18] David Bakan, Disease, Pain & Sacrifice (Chicago, IL: The University of Chicago Press, 1968), 57.

[19] C.S. Lewis, A Grief Observed (Sanfrancisco, CA: Harper Collins Publishers, Inc., 2001), 23

[20] Ibid., 45.

21 Jerry Sittser, a Grace Disguised (Grand Rapids, MI: Zondervan Publishers., 2004), 40.

22 Ibid.,74.

23 Ibid.,140.

24 Ibid., 141.

25 Ibid., 143.

26 Ibid..

27 Geoff Walter, Why Do Christians Find it Hard to Grieve (UK: Authentic Publishers, 1997),

28 Ibid.,11.

29 Juanita Bynum, The Threshing FLOOR (US: Charisma House Publishers, 2009), ix

30 Mark R. McMinn, Psychology, Theology, AND Spirituality IN CHRISTIAN COUNSELING (US: Tyndale's House Publishers, Inc.1996), 116.

31 Ibid., 117.

32 Ibid., 75.

33 Ibid., 90.

34 Mathew Edlund, M.D. The Power of Rest (New York, NY: Harper Collins Publishers, 2010). 14.15.

BIBLIOGRAPHY

Bakan, David. Pain & Sacrifice. Chicago: University of Chicago Press, 1968.

Bynum, Juanita. The Threshing FLOOR. US: Charisma House Publishers, 2009

Deits, Bob. Life after Loss: A Practical Guide to Renewing Your Life after Experiencing Major Loss, 5th Ed. Massachusetts: De Capo Press, 2009.

Edlund, Mathew. The Power of Rest. New York: Harper Collins Publishers, 2010.

Hart, Archibald D. Adrenaline, and Stress. Dallas, London, Vancouver, Melbourne: WORD PUBLISHING, 1995.

Holy Bible, New International Version. Michigan Zondervan Publishing House, 1973, 1978, 1984. www.zondervan.com.

Jones, Frank A. The Inconvenient Truths of God. California: Word of Truths Publications, 2006.

Lord, Janice Harris. "Grief and Loss." *Family Caregiver Alliance* (December 2012): http://www.caregiver.org (accessed October 20, 2014)

Lewis, C.S. A Grief Observed. California: Harper Collins Publishers, Inc., 2001.

McMinn, Mark R. Psychology, Theology, AND Spirituality IN CHRISTIAN

COUNSELING. US: Tyndale's House Publishers, Inc., 1996

Ross- Kubler, Elisabeth and Kessler, David. ON GRIEF and GRIEVING. New York: SCRIBNER, 2005.

Sittser, Jerry. A Grace Disguised. Michigan: Zondervan Publishers, 2004.

Staudacher, Carol. Men and Grief. California: New Harbinger Publications, Inc.

Tanner, Irene J. The Gift of Grief. New York: Hawthorn Books, Inc., 1976.

Walter, Geoff. Why Do Christians Find it Hard to Grieve? UK: Authentic Publishers, 1997.

Wikipedia Contributors. "Human Bonding." The Free Encyclopedia (Accessed September 10, 2014)

Wright, Norman H. Experiencing Grief. Tennessee: BEtH Publishing Group, 2004.

NOTES

NOTES

NOTES

NOTES

NOTES

NOTES

NOTES

Printed in the United States
By Bookmasters